Getting to Grips with Word Problems

**by
Colin Gallow**

**illustrated by
Robyn**

Acknowledgements
Leonie Ewing, Ian Ward and Maggie Johnson for their ideas

A QEd Publication

Published in 2009

© Colin Gallow

ISBN 978 1 898873 33 4

Published by QEd Publications, 39 Weeping Cross, Stafford ST17 0DG
Tel: 01785 620364
Fax: 01785 607797
Web site: www.qed.uk.com
Email: orders@qed.uk.com

Printed by Gutenberg Press Ltd, Malta.

Contents

Introduction

For a variety of reasons many children and young people struggle with areas of basic maths such as decimals, fractions, percentages, averages, money, measurement and so on. The difficulties are only compounded when calculations are presented in a written context, or as word problems.

This book provides a very structured route to help those who are struggling to first understand the concept and then tackle the word problem. The book starts with a number of general, but structured, word problems dealing with simple addition, subtraction, multiplication and division. The idea is to give students some early success with some simple word problems and also familiarise them with the format that is used in the book.

The sections that follow deal with specific areas such as decimals, percentages, fractions, money, averages, and measurement (area, height, length etc). The first stage comes under the sub-heading 'Getting to Grips with . . .'. This involves step-by-step activities to help improve understanding. Some sections offer just a few activities, others are more detailed. Obviously some pupils require additional support in getting to grips with certain concepts and it is up to individual teachers to try a variety of approaches to find a way of making sense of these concepts. 'Getting to Grips with . . .' is followed by a second stage called 'Solve it . . .' in which calculations are presented as word problems.

The material has been used to support children who are tackling fractions, decimals, percentages etc for the first time, but has also been used successfully to help struggling students at KS2 and KS3.

The step-by-step approach used in the book is based on the very successful *Word Problems: The Language of Mathematics* (Ewing & Ward, 2001) that is still widely used. Those who work with children and young people are well aware of how important success is in the early stages of learning. It builds confidence and turns the activity into a positive experience. As we know, all children work at very different paces, perhaps no more so than in mathematics. The step-by-step approach used in *Getting to Grips with Word Problems* will enable you to work at a pace that suits the individual child and help them to understand the structure and language of mathematical problems.

Solve It
Word problems involving addition, subtraction, multiplication and division

Students are given a word problem and then guided to finding the main elements of that problem. Using the key words for assistance, they can decide if this word problem involves addition, subtraction, multiplication or division.

They are encouraged to estimate the answer, complete the calculation and then check it.

Solve It

Mum is 38 years old and Gran is 60.

How many years older is Gran?

I have to

- add

- subtract

I have to find

- the difference in age

- the total number of years

My estimate

- More than 30

- Less than 30

My calculation

• Check it •

Solve It

Dad is 40 years old and I am 11 years old.

How many years older is Dad than me?

I have to

- add

- subtract

I have to find

- the total number of years

- the difference in age

My estimate

- More than 25

- Less than 25

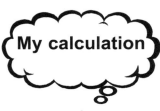

My calculation

• Check it •

Solve It

What is the difference between 25 and 6?

I have to

- add

- subtract

I have to find

- the number between the two

- how much is left after subtracting one number from the other

My estimate

- More than 15

- Less than 15

My calculation

• Check it •

Solve It

What is the difference between 147 and 62?

I have to

- add

- subtract

I have to find

- the number between the two

- how much is left after subtracting one number from the other

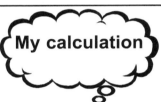 **My calculation**

 **My estimate**

- More than 75

- Less than 75

• Check it •

Solve It

Kate has 39 books. Simon has 10 times as many as Kate.

How many books does Simon have?

I have to

- add
- multiply

I have to find

- the total number of books
- the number of books Simon has got

My estimate

- More than 50
- Less than 50

My calculation

• Check it •

Solve It

Sam is 18 years old and Katie is 11 years old.

What is the difference in age between Sam and Katie?

I have to

• add

• subtract

I have to find

• the total number of years

• how many years between them

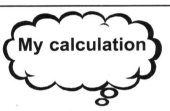

My estimate

My calculation

• More than 25

• Less than 25

• **Check it** •

Solve It

There are 125 sweets in a packet.

How many sweets are there in 5 packets?

I have to

- add

- multiply

- divide

I have to find

- the number of sweets in a packet

- the number of sweets altogether

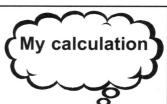
My estimate

My calculation

- More than 500

- Less than 500

• Check it •

Solve It

There are 8 classrooms in a school. In each class there are 28 children.

How many children are there in total?

I have to

- add

- multiply

- divide

I have to find

- the number of children in a class

- the total number of children altogether in the school

My estimate

- More than 200

- Less than 200

My calculation

• Check it •

Solve It

What is the product of 5 and 3?

I have to

- multiply

- subtract

- divide

I have to find

- the average

- how much you get after multiplying the two numbers together

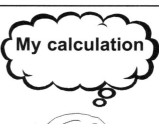
My estimate

- More than 10

- Less than 10

My calculation

• Check it •

Solve It

28 people can fit on a bus.

How many people can 4 buses carry?

I have to

- add

- multiply

- divide

I have to find

- the number of buses

- the number of people altogether in 4 buses

My estimate

- More than 100

- Less than 100

My calculation

• Check it •

Solve It

Sally reads 6 pages of a book every day.
The book has 144 pages.

How many days does he take to read the whole book?

I have to

- divide

- subtract

- multiply

I have to find

- the total number of pages in the book

- the number of days it takes to read 144 pages

My estimate

- More than 20

- Less than 20

My calculation

• Check it •

Solve It

In a factory 750 chocolates are put into boxes. Each box has 10 chocolates in it.

How many boxes will there be when all the chocolates have been put into boxes?

I have to

- subtract

- divide

- add

I have to find

- the total number of chocolates

- the total number of boxes of chocolates

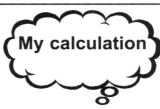

My estimate

- More than 80

- Less than 80

My calculation

• Check it •

Getting to grips with decimals

Decimals are very difficult first time around . . . and often second and third time around! When we start learning about numbers, the more digits there are, the bigger the number. Then we get to learn about decimals and the reverse can be true. It can be very perplexing . . . and some pupils really struggle to understand place value in decimals.

Decimal numbers can also be shown as fractions and percentages, and this introduces numbers and proportions of numbers. There are plenty of resources available from educational suppliers such as wall charts showing the link between fractions, decimals and percentages – the idea here is to provide a few simple examples.

It may be that you need to spend a lot more time on getting to grips with decimals before presenting them as part of a word problem. A useful method is getting pupils to devise their own questions for each other – this sometimes helps them to think a lot harder about the calculations than if they are expected to solve a problem.

Numbers and proportions

MOST

ALL

SOME

NONE

Numbers and proportions

One hundred students from the whole of Year 8 attend the school assembly.

NUMBER	PROPORTION	PERCENTAGE	FRACTION	DECIMAL NUMBER
100 students	all	100%	$\frac{1}{1}$ or 1	1.0
25 students from Tutor Group A leave the hall leaving				
75 students	three quarters	75%	$\frac{3}{4}$	0.75
25 students from Tutor Group B leave the hall leaving				
50 students	half	50%	$\frac{1}{2}$	0.5
25 students from Tutor Group C leave the hall leaving				
25 students	a quarter	25%	$\frac{1}{4}$	0.25

Getting to grips with decimals

Draw a line from the **decimal numbers** in boxes to their place on the number line.

| 5.0 | 3.6 | 0.5 | 0.9 | 2.5 |

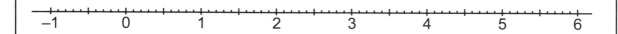

$$\frac{1}{2} \qquad 2\frac{1}{2}$$

Draw a line from the **fractions** in boxes to their place on the number line.
What can you say about those fractions and decimal numbers?

What is the <u>biggest</u> decimal number?

_____

What is the <u>smallest</u> decimal number?

_____

Getting to grips with decimals

Draw a line from the numbers in boxes to their place on the number line.

| 2.2 | | 4.7 | | 1.9 |

| 3.0 | | 0.6 | | 0.9 | | −0.3 |

```
+--+--+--+--+--+--+--+--+--+--+--+--+--+--+--+--+--+--+--+--+--+--+--+--+--+--+--+--+
  −1        0         1         2         3         4         5         6
```

What is the biggest number?

_____

What is the smallest number?

_____

Draw a line from the numbers in boxes to their place on the number line.

| 0.5 | | −0.7 | | −2.5 | | −4 |

```
+--+--+--+--+--+--+--+--+--+--+--+--+--+--+--+--+--+--+--+--+--+--+--+--+--+--+--+--+
 −5       −4        −3        −2        −1        0         1         2
```

Getting to grips with decimals

Draw a line from the numbers in boxes to their place on the number line.

| 2.0 | | 1.7 | | −1.7 |

| −2.8 | | −3.3 | | −5.0 | | −0.3 |

What is the biggest number?

_____

What is the smallest number?

_____

Draw a line from the numbers in boxes to their place on the number line.

| | −1.1 | | | 0.5 |

| −1.7 | | | −0.5 | | 1.1 |

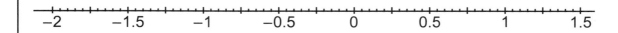

Getting to grips with decimals

Draw a line from the numbers in boxes to their place on the number line.

0.05		−0.9

−1.75		−0.75		1.25

```
├──┼──┼──┼──┼──┼──┼──┼──┤
−2    −1.5   −1   −0.5    0    0.5    1    1.5
```

What is the biggest number?

_____

What is the smallest number?

_____

Draw a line from the numbers in boxes to their place on the number line.

−0.05	1.7	0.180

−2.80	0.09	−5.0	0.4

```
├──┼──┼──┼──┼──┼──┼──┤
−5   −4   −3   −2   −1   0   1   2
```

Getting to grips with decimals

Working with decimals

4.2 + 1 = ⬚

Before writing the answer, look at the number line.

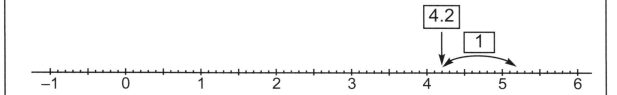

This can also be written in another way ⟶

$$+\begin{array}{r}4.2\\1.\\\hline\end{array}$$

Where the decimal point is really matters!

4.2 + .1 = ⬚

Before writing the answer, look at the number line.

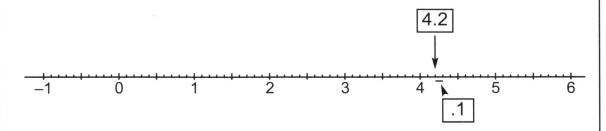

This can also be written in another way ⟶

$$+\begin{array}{r}4.2\\.1\\\hline\end{array}$$

Getting to grips with decimals

Working with decimals

3.9 + 1 = ▢

Before writing the answer, look at the number line.

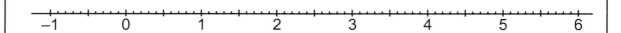

−1   0   1   2   3   4   5   6

This can also be written in another way   +

⟶   ——————

——————

Working with decimals

5.6 + 0.01 = ▢

Before writing the answer, look at the number line.

−1   0   1   2   3   4   5   6

This can also be written in another way   +

⟶   ——————

——————

Getting to grips with decimals

Working with decimals

$-1.5 + 2.5 =$ [ ]

Before writing the answer, look at the number line.

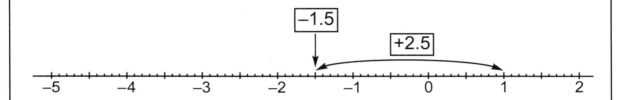

Working with decimals

$-2.5 + 3.5 - 4.0 + 2.5 =$ [ ]

Use the number line.

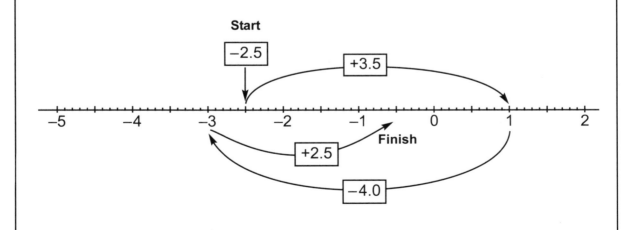

Getting to grips with decimals

Doing the calculations

12.63 – 1.02

First write it like this ⟶

$$\begin{array}{r} 12.63 \\ -\ \ 1.02 \\ \hline \\ \hline \end{array}$$

13.84 + 0.01

First write it like this ⟶

$$\begin{array}{r} + \\ \hline \\ \hline \end{array}$$

5.842 – 2.917

First write it like this ⟶

$$\begin{array}{r} - \\ \hline \\ \hline \end{array}$$

1.306 + 100.025 + 23.809

First write it like this ⟶

$$\begin{array}{r} + \\ + \\ \hline \\ \hline \end{array}$$

Getting to grips with decimals

Multiplying decimals

When multiplying a decimal number by 10, 100, 1000 etc, all we do is move the decimal point to the <u>**right**</u>. Remember, we are <u>**multiplying**</u>, so the number has to get **bigger**.

For example:

$$1.46 \times 10 = 14.6$$

The decimal number is multiplied by 10, so you move the point 1 space to the right.

$$1.46 \times 100 = 146$$

The decimal number is multiplied by 100, so you move the point 2 spaces to the right.

Now try the following calculation

$$24.372 \times 100$$

This means I have to

- move the decimal point 1 place to the right ☐

- move the decimal point 1 place to the left ☐

- move the decimal point 2 places to the right ☐

<u>**Here is my calculation**</u>

Use a calculator to check it

Getting to grips with decimals

Try the following calculation

7.7104 x 1000

This means I have to

- move the decimal point 2 places to the right ☐
- move the decimal point 1 place to the left ☐
- move the decimal point 3 places to the right ☐

Here is my calculation

• Use a calculator to check it •

Try the following calculation

17.5 x 100

This means I have to

- move the decimal point 2 places to the right ☐
- move the decimal point 1 place to the left ☐
- move the decimal point 1 place to the right ☐

Here is my calculation

• Use a calculator to check it •

Getting to grips with decimals

Dividing decimals

When dividing a decimal number by 10, 100, 1000 etc, all we do is move the decimal point to the **left**. Remember, we are **dividing**, so the number has to get **smaller**.

For example:

$186.1 \div 10 = 18.61$

The decimal number is divided by 10, so you move the point 1 space to the left.

$186.1 \div 100 = 1.861$

The decimal number is divided by 100, so you move the point 2 spaces to the left.

Now try the following calculation

$243.72 \div 100$

This means I have to

- move the decimal point 1 place to the left ☐

- move the decimal point 2 places to the left ☐

- move the decimal point 2 places to the right ☐

Here is my calculation

Use a calculator to check it

Getting to grips with decimals

Try the following calculation

771.04 ÷ 1000

This means I have to

- move the decimal point 2 places to the left ☐
- move the decimal point 3 places to the left ☐
- move the decimal point 3 places to the right ☐

Here is my calculation

• Use a calculator to check it •

Try the following calculation

17.5 ÷ 100

This means I have to

- move the decimal point 2 places to the right ☐
- move the decimal point 1 place to the left ☐
- move the decimal point 2 places to the left ☐

Here is my calculation

• Use a calculator to check it •

Solve It – decimals

Sam is 1.42 metres tall. Jane is 1.48 metres tall.

How much taller is Jane?

I have to

- add
- subtract
- divide

I have to find

- how tall Jane is
- the difference in height between Sam and Jane

My estimate

- More than 0.5 metre
- Less than 0.5 metre

My calculation

• Check it •

Solve It – decimals

A bottle of lemonade holds 0.25 litres.

If you had 4 bottles of lemonade, how many litres would that be altogether?

Tip		
1000ml	=	1 litre

I have to

- multiply

- divide

- add

I have to find

- the difference between 4 bottles

- the total amount of lemonade in four bottles

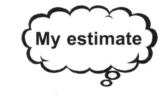

- More than 4 litres

- Less than 4 litres

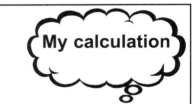

• Check it •

Solve It – decimals

Sophie weighs 40.04kg. Rob weighs 32.26kg.

They both climb onto a swing at a funfair where the maximum weight allowed is 70kg. Will the swing break with them both on it?

I have to

• add

• subtract

• multiply

I have to find

• the difference in their weight

• the total of Sophie and Rob's weight

My estimate

• More than 70kg

• Less than 70kg

My calculation

• Check it •

Solve It – decimals

A rope 4 metres long is cut into pieces 0.5 metres long.

How many pieces of rope will there be?

I have to

- divide

- subtract

- multiply

I have to find

- the number of 0.5 metre pieces in a 4 metre length of rope

- the length of the rope

My estimate

- More than 10

- Less than 10

My calculation

• Check it •

Solve It – decimals

You have to build a wall 2 metres long. You don't have enough bricks and when you finish you find the wall is 45cm short.

How long is the finished wall?

I have to

- divide

- subtract

- multiply

I have to find

- how many times 45cm goes into 2 metres

- the length of wall

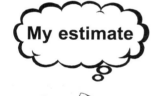
My estimate

- More than 1 metre

- Less than 1 metre

My calculation

• Check it •

Getting to grips with percentages

A percentage (like a fraction), is a very difficult concept when first visited. For those who do not fully grasp the idea of proportion, it becomes a confusing mystery.

Pages 19 and 20, introducing the concept of proportion, are used again to help reinforce the links between percentages and fractions.

Like fractions, spend a lot of time on getting to grips with percentages. A useful way of getting to grips with the concept is to let pupils walk around the school in pairs asking each other to estimate percentages – such as what percentage of a wall has windows, for example or what percentage of the hall does the stage take up?

Numbers and proportions

MOST

This is a **large percentage** of all of the characters in the group

ALL

This is **100 percent** of all of the characters in the group

SOME

This is a **small percentage** of all of the characters in the group

NONE

This is **zero percent** of all of the characters in the group

Numbers and proportions

Ten thousand (10,000) people attend a heavy metal music festival.

NUMBER	PROPORTION	PERCENTAGE	FRACTION	DECIMAL NUMBER
10,000 people The organisers estimate that 7,500 of those that attend are male	all	100%	$\frac{1}{1}$ or 1	1.0
7,500 males 5,000 of the fans use public transport to get to the venue	three quarters	75%	$\frac{3}{4}$	0.75
5,000 fans The organisers estimate that 2,500 of those that attend are female	half	50%	$\frac{1}{2}$	0.5
2,500 females	a quarter	25%	$\frac{1}{4}$	0.25

Getting to grips with percentages

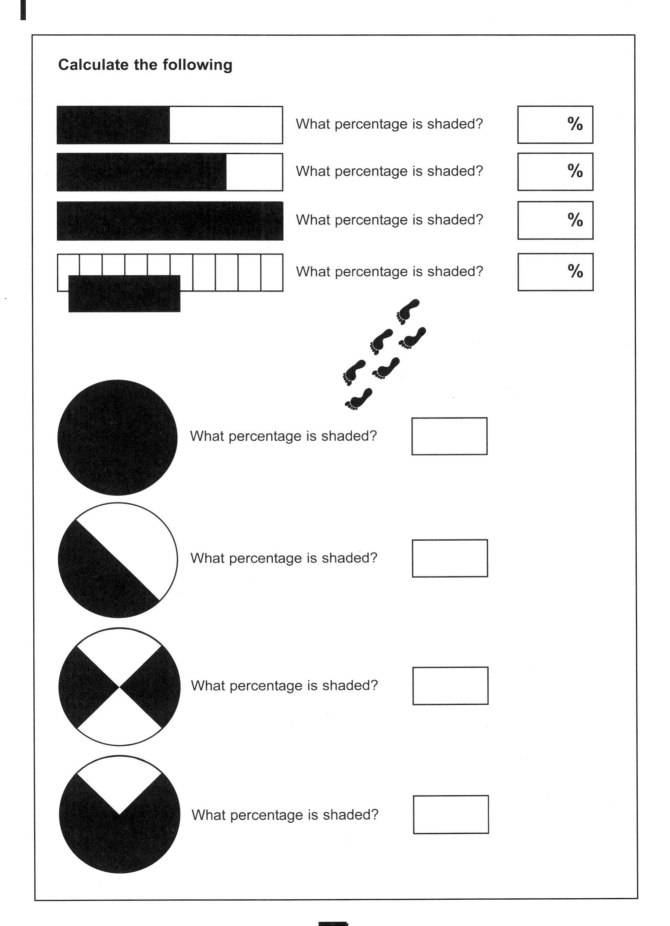

Calculate the following

What percentage is shaded? [ ] %

What percentage is shaded? [ ] %

What percentage is shaded? [ ] %

What percentage is shaded? [ ] %

What percentage is shaded? [ ]

What percentage is shaded? [ ]

What percentage is shaded? [ ]

What percentage is shaded? [ ]

Getting to grips with percentages

Working out a percentage of a number

These questions are sometimes asked like this:

What is 10% of £25?   You need to write this in another way.

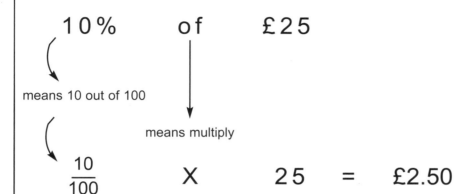

So **10% of £25 is £2.50**

Now try the following calculation

What is 15% of £25?

This means I have to

- work out $\frac{15}{100}$ X 25

My guess for the answer is

between £3 and £5 ☐

between £10 and £20 ☐

between £30 and £40 ☐

Here is my calculation

Use a calculator to check it

Getting to grips with percentages

Working out a percentage of a number

Sometimes you will be asked to work out a percentage like this:

You have £50 and spend £10. What is this as a percentage of £50?

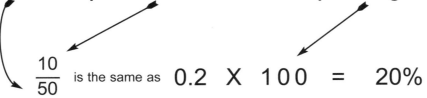

$\dfrac{10}{50}$ is the same as $0.2 \times 100 = 20\%$

So £10 is 20% of £50   check it →

£10 20%	£10 20%	£10 20%	£10 20%	£10 20%

Now try the following calculation

Sue spends £7 on make up. What is this as a percentage of £25?

This means I have to

- work out

  ⎯⎯ is the same as [ ] X 100

My guess for the answer is

between 20 and 30%   [ ]

between 40 and 50%   [ ]

between 50 and 60%   [ ]

Here is my calculation

Use a calculator to check it

Getting to grips with percentages

Working out percentage change

Sometimes you will be asked to work out something like this:

You buy a mobile phone for £50 and sell it for £65.
What is your percentage profit?

What you sold it for (65) minus what you paid (£50) → $\dfrac{15}{50}$ X 1 0 0 = 30%

What you paid →

So you have made 30% profit on the deal.

Now try the following calculation

Sol spends £24 on an old painting. He sells it for £48. What is his % profit?

This means I have to

- work out

$$— \text{ X } 100 \quad \boxed{}$$

My guess for the answer is

between 20 and 40% $\boxed{}$

between 40 and 60% $\boxed{}$

between 60 and 80% $\boxed{}$

Here is my calculation

Use a calculator to check it

Solve It – percentages

In a class of 30 pupils, 40% of the children are girls.

How many girls are there in the class?

Reminder
See the example on page 42.

This means I have to

- work out what 40% of 30 is

$$\frac{}{100} \quad X$$

My estimate

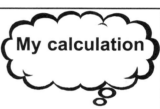

My calculation

Now you can also calculate how many *boys* there are in the class.

- More than 10

- Less than 10

• Check it •

Solve It – percentages

In a class of 40 pupils, 26 of the children are boys.

What percentage of the class are boys?

Reminder
See the example on page 43.

This means I have to

- work out

  —— is the same as [ ] X 100

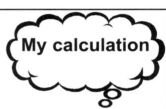

My estimate

My calculation

- More than 60%

- Less than 60%

• Check it •

Solve It – percentages

Stuart's weight is 50kg. His weight increased by 10%.

What is his new weight?

Reminder
See the example on page 42.

This means I have to

- work out what 10% of 50 is

$$\overline{100} \quad X$$

Then I have to

- add that to what he used to weigh (50kg)

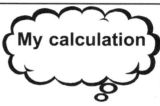

My calculation

My estimate

- More than 60kg

- Less than 60kg

• Check it •

Solve It – percentages

In a maths test with 100 questions, Kate got 70 questions correct.

What percentage mark did she get for the test?

Reminder
See the example on page 43.

I have to find

- how many questions there were in the maths test

- the mark in % that Kate got

This means I have to

- work out

  —— is the same as ☐ X 100

My estimate

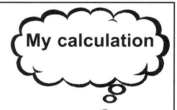

My calculation

- More than 50%

- Less than 50%

• Check it •

Solve It – percentages

In a maths test there are 75 questions.
Ishan got 60 of the questions correct.

What percentage mark did he get for the test?

Reminder
See the example on page 43.

I have to find

- how many questions there were in the maths test

- the mark in % that Ishan got

This means I have to

- **work out**

  —— is the same as [ ] X 100

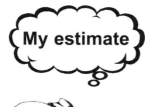

My estimate

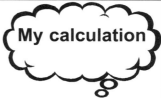

My calculation

- More than 75%

- Less than 60%

• Check it •

Solve It – percentages

Jane ate 40% of a cake and Sam ate 30% of the cake.

What percentage of the cake was left?

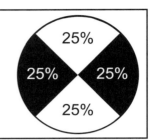

I have to find

- how much of the cake was left

- how much cake was eaten

I have to

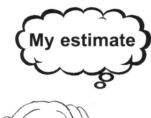
My estimate

- More than 70%

- Less than 50%

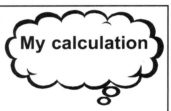
My calculation

• Check it •

Solve It – percentages

Reminder
See the example on page 42.

A baby weighs 10kg. Her weight drops by 5%.

What is the baby's weight now?

This means I have to

- work out what 5% of 10 is

$$\overline{}_{100} \quad X$$

Then I have to

- subtract that from what the baby used to weigh (10kg)

My estimate

My calculation

- More than 8kg

- Less than 7kg

• Check it •

Solve It – percentages

Reminder
See the example on page 42.

Amelie's weight increases from 10kg over a number of months by 100%.

What is Amelie's weight now?

This means I have to

- work out

Then I have to

- add that to . . .

My estimate

- More than 15kg

- Less than 15kg

My calculation

• Check it •

Solve It – percentages

There is a 35% discount offer on music CDs that normally cost £14.

How much discount is that in pounds?

Reminder
See the example on page 42.

This means I have to

- work out

Then I have to

- add that to . . .

- subtract that from . . .

My estimate

- More than £5

- Less than £5

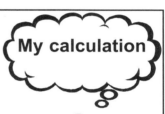

My calculation

• Check it •

Solve It – percentages

There is a 30% discount on all DVDs that normally cost £20.

What is the new price?

Reminder
See the example on page 42.

This means I have to

- work out

Then I have to

- add that to . . .

- subtract that from . . .

My estimate

- More than £15

- Less than £15

My calculation

• Check it •

Solve It – percentages

You've got a job in a bookshop. There are 400 Harry Potter books in stock, but 10% of them were damaged during delivery and will have to be sold at a discount.

How many are damaged?

I have to find

- how many Harry Potter books there are ☐

- what the discount is going to be ☐

- how many damaged books there are ☐

This means I have to

- work out

My guess for the answer is

between 10 and 30 ☐

between 30 and 50 ☐

between 60 and 80 ☐

Here is my calculation

Use a calculator to check it

Solve It – percentages

You've got a job in a sports shop. There are 120 England football shirts in stock. 30% of them are red, the rest are white.
The shop manager tells you to make up SPECIAL OFFER stickers for the white shirts because they aren't selling well.

How many will you have to make up?

I have to find

• what the special offer price is ☐

• how many white shirts there are ☐

• the number of shirts altogether ☐

This means I have to

• work out 30% of 120 to find out how many red shirts there are; and then I can work out how many white shirts there are

My guess for the answer is

between 10 and 50 ☐

between 50 and 70 ☐

between 70 and 100 ☐

Here is my calculation

Use a calculator to check it

Getting to grips with fractions

Understanding the concept of fractions can be very difficult to get to grips with, let alone manipulate the numbers. As in the previous sections on decimals and percentages, this section starts by introducing the concept of proportion to help reinforce the links between fractions, percentages and decimals before presenting word problems.

A very useful resource for practising fractions is *Target Maths* (Set 4) by Ian Ward, available from QEd Publications. These cards provide an excellent opportunity for reinforcing these skills.

Numbers and proportions

Fifty thousand (50,000) people attend a football match between Liverpool and Arsenal.

NUMBER	PROPORTION	PERCENTAGE	FRACTION	DECIMAL NUMBER
50,000 people	all	100%	$\frac{1}{1}$ or 1	1.0
37,500 are Arsenal supporters				
37,500 Arsenal supporters	three quarters	75%	$\frac{3}{4}$	0.75
25,000 of the fans use public transport to get to the venue				
25,000 fans	half	50%	$\frac{1}{2}$	0.5
Statistics show that 12,500 of those that attend are under 18 years old				
12,500 are under 18 years old	a quarter	25%	$\frac{1}{4}$	0.25

There are 2 equal parts to this rectangle

What **fraction** of the rectangle is shaded?

The answer is **1 out of 2 parts** or, written another way $\frac{1}{2}$

Calculate the following

What **fraction** of the rectangle is shaded?

The answer is ___ **out of** ___ **parts** or, written another way

What **fraction** of the rectangle is shaded?

The answer is ___ **out of** ___ **parts** or, written another way

What **fraction** of the rectangle is shaded?

The answer is ___ **out of** ___ **parts** or, written another way

Getting to grips with fractions

Calculate the following

If you moved the shaded block into line with the rectangle, what **fraction** of the rectangle is shaded?

The answer is ___ **out of** ___ **parts** or, written another way

If you moved the shaded block into line with the rectangle, what **fraction** of the rectangle is shaded?

The answer is ___ **out of** ___ **parts** or, written another way

What **fraction** of the rectangle is shaded?

The answer is ___ **out of** ___ **parts** or, written another way

Estimate what **fraction** of the rectangle is shaded? (One way is to divide it yourself into equal parts).

The answer is ___ **out of** ___ **parts** or, written another way

Getting to grips with fractions

Calculate the following

What fraction of the circle is shaded?

What **percentage** is that?

What **fraction** is shaded?

What **percentage** is that?

What **fraction** is shaded?

What **percentage** is that?

What **fraction** is shaded?

What **percentage** is that?

Getting to grips with fractions

Did you know that $\dfrac{1}{2}$ is the same as $\dfrac{2}{4}$?

Shade in $\dfrac{1}{2}$ of the rectangle

Shade in $\dfrac{2}{4}$ of the rectangle

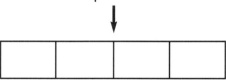

Use the boxes below to help you

$\dfrac{2}{6}$ is the same as $\dfrac{\square}{3}$

$\dfrac{5}{10}$ is the same as $\dfrac{\square}{2}$

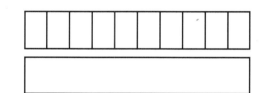

$\dfrac{3}{9} = \dfrac{\square}{3}$

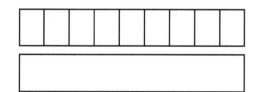

$\dfrac{1}{4} = \dfrac{\square}{16}$

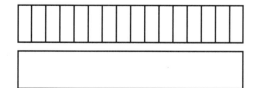

$\dfrac{3}{5} = \dfrac{\square}{20}$

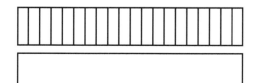

Getting to grips with fractions

Write in the missing numbers

50% = $\dfrac{\boxed{}}{2}$ Shade this in ⟶ [ ]

100% = $\dfrac{\boxed{}}{2}$ Shade this in ⟶ [ ]

75% = $\dfrac{\boxed{}}{4}$ Shade this in ⟶ [| | |]

25% = $\dfrac{\boxed{}}{4}$ Shade this in ⟶ [ ]

Estimating

Estimate $\dfrac{1}{2}$ of the rectangle and shade it in   [ ]

What percentage do you think $\dfrac{1}{2}$ is?   [ ]

Estimate $\dfrac{1}{3}$ of the rectangle and shade it in   [ ]

What percentage do you think $\dfrac{1}{3}$ is?   [ ]

Estimate $\dfrac{3}{5}$ of the rectangle and shade it in   [ ]

What percentage do you think $\dfrac{3}{5}$ is?   [ ]

Getting to grips with fractions

Mixed fractions

$\dfrac{4}{3}$ is a **top heavy** fraction because the number on **top** is **bigger** than the number below. This can be converted to a <u>mixed fraction</u>.

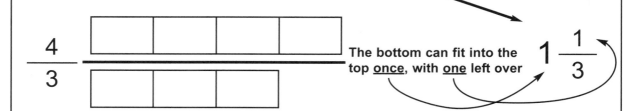

$\dfrac{4}{3}$ The bottom can fit into the top <u>once</u>, with <u>one</u> left over $1\dfrac{1}{3}$

Here is another example

$\dfrac{5}{2}$ The bottom can fit into the top <u>twice</u>, with one left over $2\dfrac{1}{2}$

Try converting these fractions

$\dfrac{3}{2}$ The bottom can fit into the top _____, with _____ left over

$\dfrac{5}{3}$ The bottom can fit into the top _____, with _____ left over

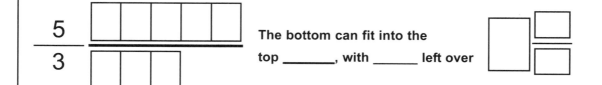

Getting to grips with fractions

$\dfrac{7}{2}$ The bottom can fit into the top _____, with _____ left over

Now convert these fractions without the rectangles

$\dfrac{9}{4} = 2\dfrac{\square}{4}$

$\dfrac{15}{4} =$

$\dfrac{20}{3} =$

$\dfrac{19}{2} =$

Getting to grips with fractions

Complete the fractions

and write these numbers

$2\frac{1}{2} = \dfrac{5}{2}$

For example

Two and a half

$3\frac{1}{2} = \dfrac{\square}{2}$

$4\frac{1}{3} = \dfrac{\square}{3}$

$2\frac{1}{3} = \dfrac{\square}{3}$

$2\frac{1}{4} = \dfrac{\square}{4}$

$4\frac{1}{4} = \dfrac{\square}{4}$

$1\frac{2}{3} = \dfrac{\square}{3}$

$2\frac{3}{4} = \dfrac{\square}{4}$

$6\frac{2}{3} = \dfrac{\square}{3}$

$7\frac{3}{4} = \dfrac{\square}{4}$

Getting to grips with fractions

Which of the following fractions is the same as a half?

$\frac{4}{8}$ $\frac{3}{6}$ $\frac{5}{10}$ $\frac{6}{12}$

$\frac{30}{60}$ $\frac{7}{14}$

$\frac{2}{5}$ $\frac{3}{9}$

Which of the following fractions is the same as a quarter?

$\frac{3}{24}$ $\frac{8}{32}$

$\frac{4}{16}$ $\frac{3}{12}$

$\frac{2}{10}$ $\frac{2}{8}$

$\frac{5}{20}$ $\frac{8}{16}$

Which of the following fractions is the same as a third?

$\frac{3}{21}$ $\frac{4}{12}$

$\frac{6}{12}$ $\frac{2}{6}$

$\frac{3}{9}$ $\frac{6}{18}$

$\frac{5}{15}$ $\frac{6}{24}$

Solve It – fractions

Maggie carries out a survey of her class of 20 to find out how many wear glasses. She wants to compare her year group to others in the school. She finds that 0.25 of her class wear glasses.

What fraction of her class wear glasses?

I have to find

- how many students wear glasses ☐
- what fraction of the class wear glasses ☐
- Maggie's glasses ☐

This means I have to

- work out 0.25 of 20 ☐
- multiply 0.25 by 20 ☐
- convert 0.25 into a fraction ☐

My guess for the answer is

about 5 ☐

about $\frac{1}{3}$ ☐

about $\frac{1}{4}$ ☐

Here is my calculation

How can you check it?

Solve It – fractions

In a class of 30 students, $\frac{1}{3}$ stay on at school; $\frac{1}{3}$ go to college, and the rest get jobs.

How many students went on to college?

I have to find

- how many students stayed in education ☐

- what percentage went to college ☐

- how many went to college ☐

This means I have to

- work out $\frac{1}{3}$ of 30

My guess for the answer is

between 5 and 10 ☐

between 11 and 15 ☐

between 16 and 20 ☐

Here is my calculation

How can you check it?

Solve It – fractions

Simon buys a new pair of jeans for £30. On his way home he sees the same style of jeans in another shop having a sale and there is $\frac{1}{3}$ off the original price.

How much would he have paid if he'd bought the jeans in the sale?

I have to find

- how much he would save ☐
- what the discount price is ☐
- which shop is having a sale ☐

This means I have to

My guess for the answer is

between £5 and £10 ☐

between £10 and £15 ☐

between £15 and £20 ☐

Here is my calculation

How can you check it?

Solve It – fractions

A family of four go on holiday to Canada one year and Greece the following year. They find that the holiday to Greece is a fraction of the cost of the Canadian holiday.

In total, they spent £4000 on the holiday to Canada and only £1000 on the trip to Greece.

What fraction of the Canadian trip did the Greek holiday cost?

I have to find

• the cost of a holiday to Canada ☐

• how much more expensive the Canadian holiday was ☐

• the difference (as a fraction) in cost between the holidays ☐

This means I have to

My guess for the answer is

$\frac{1}{3}$ ☐

$\frac{1}{4}$ ☐

$\frac{1}{2}$ ☐

Here is my calculation

How can you check it?

Solve It – fractions

The roads around a school in the mornings are very busy. Jodie is asked to do a survey of the number of students who are taken to school by car. After a week collecting information, Jodie can show that 75% of the children arrive at the school by car.

What is this as a fraction?

I have to find

- how many students use transport ☐

- why the roads are so busy ☐

- what fraction uses cars to get to school ☐

This means I have to

- convert 75% into a fraction ☐

- make students walk to school ☐

- convert 0.75 into a percentage ☐

My guess for the answer is

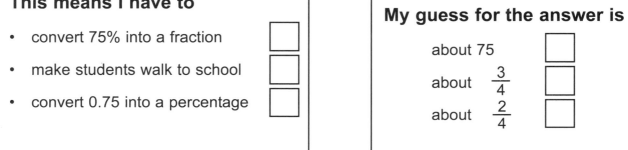

about 75 ☐

about $\frac{3}{4}$ ☐

about $\frac{2}{4}$ ☐

Here is my calculation

How can you check it?

Solve It – fractions

At another school nearby with 600 students, they have been encouraged to use bicycles to get to school. The scheme is very successful and on average 400 students cycle to school.

What fraction of the total cycles to school?

I have to find

- what fraction of students cycle to school ☐

- the total number of bicycles ☐

- how many students are lazy ☐

This means I have to

- convert 600 into a fraction ☐

- subtract 400 from 600 ☐

- work out what fraction 400 is of 600 ☐

My guess for the answer is

about 200 ☐

about $\frac{1}{4}$ ☐

about $\frac{2}{3}$ ☐

Here is my calculation

How can you check it?

Solve It – fractions

Sam, Josh and Sarah order a large pizza for £12 and each person eats $\frac{1}{3}$.
Josh hasn't got any money with him, but Sam agrees to pay for his share.

How much do Sam and Sarah pay?

I have to find

- how much pizza Josh eats ☐
- $\frac{1}{3}$ of £12 ☐
- $\frac{2}{3}$ of £12 ☐

This means I have to

My guess for the answer is

Sam pays ☐

Sarah pays ☐

Here is my calculation

How can you check it?

Getting to grips with money

For most of us, money is so much a part of our lives from an early age that understanding and using currency is never a problem. However, when presented with a word problem involving money, many begin to struggle. From a functional maths point of view it is very important that young people understand interest rates, how to calculate simple profit and loss, discounts and so on.

In this section, therefore, after a few introductory steps covering the addition and subtraction of money, the focus is on solving word problems.

If the pupils/students you are working with need further support with the initial steps, a very useful resource is *Quick Cards: Time, Money, Approximation and Estimation* by Robert Thompson, published by QEd Publications.

Getting to grips with money

Calculate the following

Write £2.30 in pence

Write 415p in pounds and pence

Write 705p in pounds and pence

Write £125 in words

Write £3420 in words

Write £7015 in words

£5.30 + 75p

£7.00 − £4.64

36p x 12

£5.30 ÷ 10

£16.80 ÷ 6

£328 ÷ 4

Solve It – money

Lee and Brandon go to the cinema. The tickets cost £5.50 each.
Lee pays for the tickets with a £20 note.

How much change does Lee get back?

I have to find

- how much two tickets cost ☐

- the difference between £20 and £5.50 ☐

- £20 minus the cost of two tickets ☐

This means I have to

- add £5.50 and £5.50

- subtract that from £20

My guess for the answer is

between £4 and £9 ☐

between £10 and £15 ☐

between £15 and £17 ☐

Rounding
Number Shark
Decimals
→ rounding

Here is my calcula[tion]

How can you check it?

Solve It – money

Kate buys the following items:

1) a football (£5.99)
2) some shin pads (£9.99)
3) a pair of thick socks (£6.99)

She hands over £30.

How much change does Kate get back?

This means I have to

My guess for the answer is

between £2 and £5 ☐

between £6 and £10 ☐

between £11 and £15 ☐

Here is my calculation

How can you check it?

Solve It – money

Jade is given £300 by an aunt. She decides to put it in the bank and earn some interest on it. The bank offers her 5% interest per annum.

At the end of the year how much interest will she have earned?

This means I have to

My guess for the answer is

between £2 and £5 ☐

between £6 and £10 ☐

between £11 and £15 ☐

Here is my calculation

How can you check it?

Solve It – money

Mark has saved £56 from doing his paper round. He decides to spend it on computer games. He finds some second-hand deals where they cost £15 each.

Estimate how many games he will be able to buy.

Estimate how much money he will have left over after he has paid.

Estimate how much money he will need to earn to buy one more game.

Here are my calculations

How can you check it?

Solve It – money

Steve buys an old bicycle for £20, fixes it and sells it on ebay for £36.

What **percentage profit** did he make?

Reminder
See the example on page 44.

This means I have to

My guess for the answer is

between 70% and 90% ☐

between 50% and 70% ☐

between 10% and 30% ☐

Here is my calculation

How can you check it?

Solve It – money

Oliver gets a holiday job in the local greengrocer shop and is given the following price list.

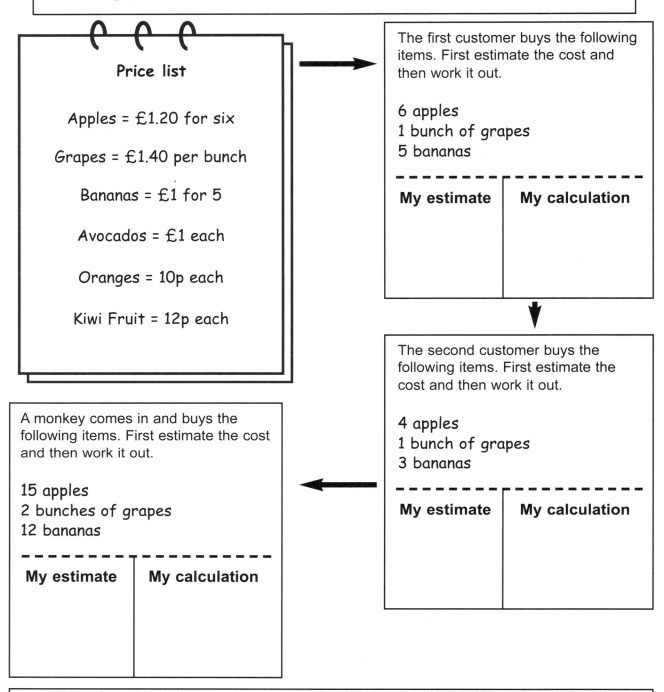

Price list

Apples = £1.20 for six

Grapes = £1.40 per bunch

Bananas = £1 for 5

Avocados = £1 each

Oranges = 10p each

Kiwi Fruit = 12p each

The first customer buys the following items. First estimate the cost and then work it out.

6 apples
1 bunch of grapes
5 bananas

My estimate	My calculation

The second customer buys the following items. First estimate the cost and then work it out.

4 apples
1 bunch of grapes
3 bananas

My estimate	My calculation

A monkey comes in and buys the following items. First estimate the cost and then work it out.

15 apples
2 bunches of grapes
12 bananas

My estimate	My calculation

At the end of the day, everything is reduced to half price. What would you pay for the following?

12 apples
3 bunches of grapes
4 bananas
2 oranges
2 avocado pears

My calculation

Solve It – money

Del opens a small shop selling fruit and vegetables. He buys 50 lettuces at 50p each. He works out that he needs to price them so that he makes a 60% profit on each lettuce.

What price does he charge for each lettuce?

Reminder
See the example on page 42.

This means I have to

My guess for the answer is

between 50p and 60p ☐

between 70p and 80p ☐

between 90p and 95p ☐

Here is my calculation

How can you check it?

Del sells 30 of the lettuces at this price, but they begin to get soft and he decides to sell off the rest at just 20% profit. He sells all the lettuces.

What profit does he make on the sale of all the lettuces?

Here is my calculation

How can you check it?

Solve It – money

Richard gets his first job and is told he will earn £11,000 per year.
He makes a list of his main expenses per month to see if his income will cover these.

Will he earn more in his job than he spends on his main expenses?

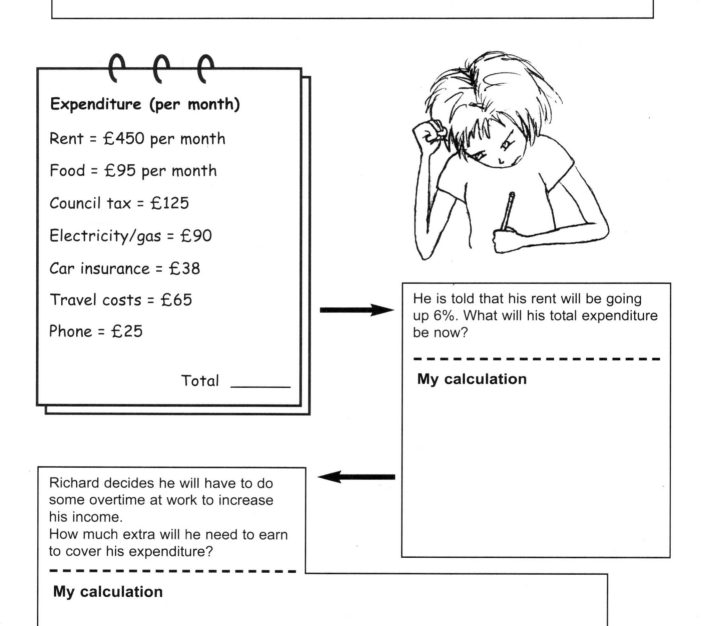

Expenditure (per month)

Rent = £450 per month

Food = £95 per month

Council tax = £125

Electricity/gas = £90

Car insurance = £38

Travel costs = £65

Phone = £25

Total _____

He is told that his rent will be going up 6%. What will his total expenditure be now?

- - - - - - - - - - - - - - - - - - -

My calculation

Richard decides he will have to do some overtime at work to increase his income.
How much extra will he need to earn to cover his expenditure?

- - - - - - - - - - - - - - - - - - -

My calculation

Getting to grips with mean, median, mode, range

The terms 'mean', 'median', 'mode' and 'range' don't have any meaning to pupils which is why they often cause difficulties . . . and yet in tests they are often some of the easiest marks. Especially for pupils who struggle with maths, here are some activities that can look complicated (because of the lists of numbers often presented), but by following simple steps can easily be unravelled.

Getting to grips with mode

Finding the **MODE** is really simple . . . it's just the most **common** number . . . the number that appears most often.

1, 2, 2, 2, 3, 4, 4, 6, 8, 8, 10, 10	There are more 2s than other numbers . . . so **2** is the **mode**.

Look at the numbers below. What is the mode?

1   1   2   2   4   4   4   6   8   8   10   10

I have to find

- the total

- the modal value

I have to

- add the numbers

- count each number

My answer

Now try the following

3, 5, 3, 0, 3, 5, 7, 3, 4, 6, 4, 5   What is the mode?

-3, 1, 13, 0, -5, 9, 2, -3, 7, 6, 3, 5   What is the mode?

Solve It – mode

Look at the following coins.

What is the mode?

I have to find

- the average ☐

- the difference between the coins ☐

- the most common value ☐

This means I have to

My answer is

Solve It – mode

Look at the following list showing monthly temperatures.

	Jan	Feb	Mar	Apr	May	June	July	Aug	Sept	Oct	Nov	Dec
Temperatures ^{o}C	12	13	17	20	24	27	28	27	25	21	16	13

What is the mode?

I have to find

- the hottest month ☐

- the temperature that occurs the most number of times ☐

- the difference between the hottest and coldest month ☐

This means I have to

My answer is

Getting to grips with median

Finding the **MEDIAN** is really simple . . . all you need to do is **rearrange the numbers in order**, and then find the middle value.

Look at the numbers below

1 4 2 1 6 -4 1 7 -2 0 10 9 2

Rearrange the numbers, the smallest number first

-4 -2 0 1 1 1 2 2 4 6 7 9 10

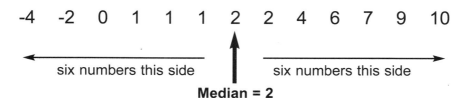

← six numbers this side   six numbers this side →

Median = 2

What if the numbers don't work out so easily?
Look at the numbers below

3 7 4 9 6 -7 1 8 -2 3 11 9 0 12

Rearrange the numbers, the smallest number first

-7 -2 0 1 3 3 4 6 7 8 9 9 11 12

← seven numbers this side   seven numbers this side →

Median = 5 (the number between **4** and **6**)

Solve It – median

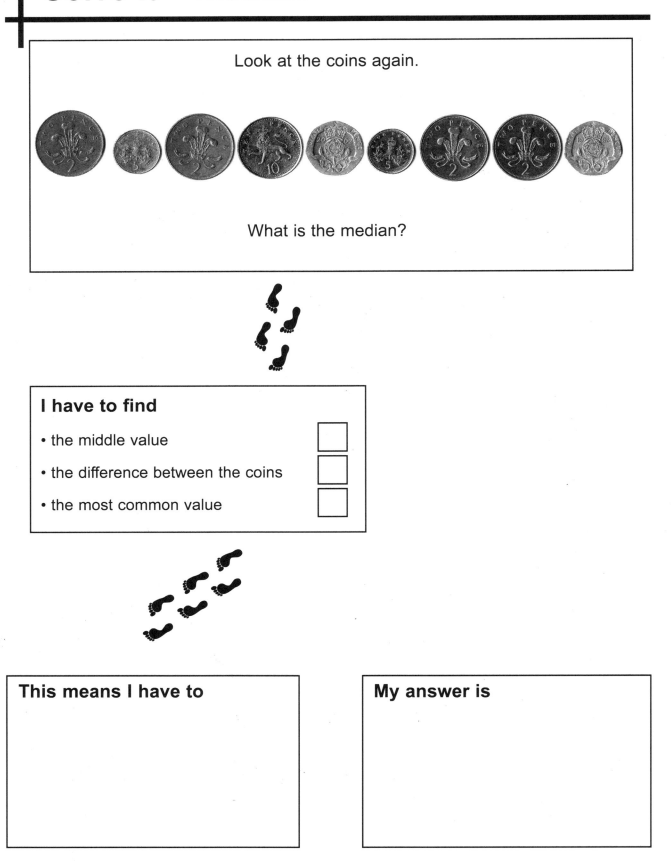

Look at the coins again.

What is the median?

I have to find

- the middle value ☐
- the difference between the coins ☐
- the most common value ☐

This means I have to

My answer is

Solve It – median

Look at the list of monthly temperatures again.

	Jan	Feb	Mar	Apr	May	June	July	Aug	Sept	Oct	Nov	Dec
Temperatures °C	12	13	17	20	24	27	28	27	25	21	16	13

What is the median?

I have to find

- the difference between the hottest and coldest month ☐

- the temperature that occurs the most number of times ☐

- the middle value ☐

This means I have to	My answer is

Getting to grips with mean

Finding the **MEAN** is the same as working out the **average**.

Look at the 7 numbers below

3   5   3   2   7   5   10

Add them all together and you get a **total** of **35**

There are 7 numbers, so **divide** the **total** by **7**

35 ÷ 7 = 5

The average or mean is 5

Imagine you do four maths tests and get the following marks out of 10.

5   8   6   5

What is your mean (average) mark out of 10?

This means I have to

My answer is

Solve It – mean

Look at the monthly rainfall in Mumbai, India's largest city.

	Jan	Feb	Mar	Apr	May	June	July	Aug	Sept	Oct	Nov	Dec
Rainfall in mm	5	5	0	0	20	480	610	340	260	50	16	0

What is the mean annual rainfall in Mumbai?

I have to find

- the difference between the wettest and driest month ☐

- the average rainfall for the year ☐

- the total amount of rainfall in Mumbai ☐

This means I have to

My answer is

Further activities dealing with solving problems involving averages can be found on pages 97-104.

Getting to grips with range

Finding the **RANGE** is also simple . . . **rearrange the numbers in order**, and then find the **difference** between the **highest** and **lowest** values.

Look at the numbers below

1   4   2   1   6   1   7   10   9   2

Rearrange the numbers, the smallest number first

1   1   1   2   2   4   6   7   9   10

The highest value is **10**
The lowest value is **1**

Calculate the **difference** between these
10 − 1 = 9

So the **range** is 9

Bill records the outside temperature throughout the day. Here is his list.

−2   0   1   3   7   9   5   4   4   2

What was the **range** of temperature for the day?

This means I have to

My answer is

Solve It – range

Look again at the monthly rainfall in Mumbai.

	Jan	Feb	Mar	Apr	May	June	July	Aug	Sept	Oct	Nov	Dec
Rainfall in mm	5	5	0	0	20	480	610	340	260	50	16	0

What is the annual range of rainfall in Mumbai?

I have to find

- the total amount of rainfall in Mumbai ☐
- the difference between the highest and lowest values ☐
- the average rainfall for the year ☐

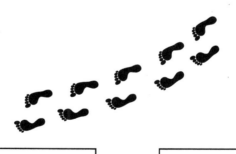

This means I have to

My answer is

Solve It – range

Look at the list of monthly temperatures again.

	Jan	Feb	Mar	Apr	May	June	July	Aug	Sept	Oct	Nov	Dec
Temperatures °C	12	13	17	20	24	27	28	27	25	21	16	13

What is the annual range of temperature?

I have to find

- the difference between the hottest and coldest month ☐

- the temperature that occurs the most number of times ☐

- the average temperature ☐

This means I have to

My answer is

Getting to grips with averages

On pages 92 and 93 there are some steps to help pupils get to grips with mean (average).

In this section, the focus is on solving word problems dealing with averages.

Solve It – averages

Stuart wrote 4 maths tests and got the following marks out of 10.

5   8   6   5

What is Stuart's average for the tests?

This means I have to

1) Add the numbers together

2) Then divide the total by the number of tests.

Here is my calculation

Use a calculator to check it

Solve It – averages

At a bookshop you buy 8 books at £1 each and 2 books at £6 each.

What is the average cost of a book?

This means I have to

Here is my calculation

Use a calculator to check it

Solve It – averages

You buy 5 bottles of cola at a cost of £2 each and 5 bottles of lemonade at a cost of £3 each.

What is the average cost of a bottle?

This means I have to

Here is my calculation

Use a calculator to check it

Solve It – averages

Below is a list of a group of friends and their ages.

Stuart	12
Simon	11
Lucy	13
Jansha	15
Peter	14

What is the average age of the group?

This means I have to

Here is my calculation

Use a calculator to check it

Solve It – averages

A group of friends did a walk to raise funds for charity.
As a group they were sponsored 50p a mile.
Below is a list of the distances each person walked.

Sam	8 miles
Kate	4 miles
Jo	9 miles
Helen	5 miles
Des	10 miles
Lee	6 miles

How much money did the group raise for charity?

This means I have to

Here is my calculation

Use a calculator to check it

Draw a graph showing the distances walked by each person.

Solve It – averages

A car travels 100 miles in 2 hours.

What is its average speed?

This means I have to

Here is my calculation

Use a calculator to check it

How many miles will it travel in 3 hours?

Here is my calculation

Use a calculator to check it

Solve It – averages

Before you go on holiday you calculate that the journey is 280 miles.

If you can travel at an average speed of 70 miles per hour, how long will the journey take?

This means I have to

My guess for the answer is

210 hours ☐

4 hours ☐

6 hours ☐

Here is my calculation

How can you check it?

Getting to grips with measurement
Length, Height, Area, Perimeter, Volume, Weight, Time

Units of measurement are difficult for pupils to get their heads around . . . they need to get a 'feel' for distances, height, weight etc before they can get their heads around calculations. The emphasis in the early steps here is on estimating.

Take advantage of random opportunities . . . like picking up a stapler and asking 'do you think this is heavier than a cup of coffee?' or 'how far do you think it is to the hall from here?' Because the answer required is not exact, pupils with difficulties feel more comfortable about trying and so there's a much better chance of helping them understand and become familiar with the language.

Getting to grips with length

Calculating length

What is the length (in mm) of a pen?

What is the length (in metres) of your bed?

What is the length (in metres) of your classroom?

What is the length (in mm) of a mobile phone?

How far is it (in km) from your home to school?

How many metres is the length of the school hall?

Calculate some large distances

How many km is it to Paris?

How many miles is it to New York?

How many miles is it to Beijing?

You can check your answers on www.freemaptools.com

Getting to grips with height

Estimate the height of a door in the school. What is the nearest measurement?

10cm	50cm	100cm	2m	10m

Now measure the height of the door

What is the height (in metres) of your maths teacher?

What is the height (in mm) of a coffee cup?

What is the height (in mm) of a mobile phone?

What is the height (in metres) of your classroom?

Estimate the height (in metres) of a house that you can see

Find out some great heights

How high is the Empire State Building in New York?

How high is Mt Everest?

How high do passenger aeroplanes normally fly?

Getting to grips with area

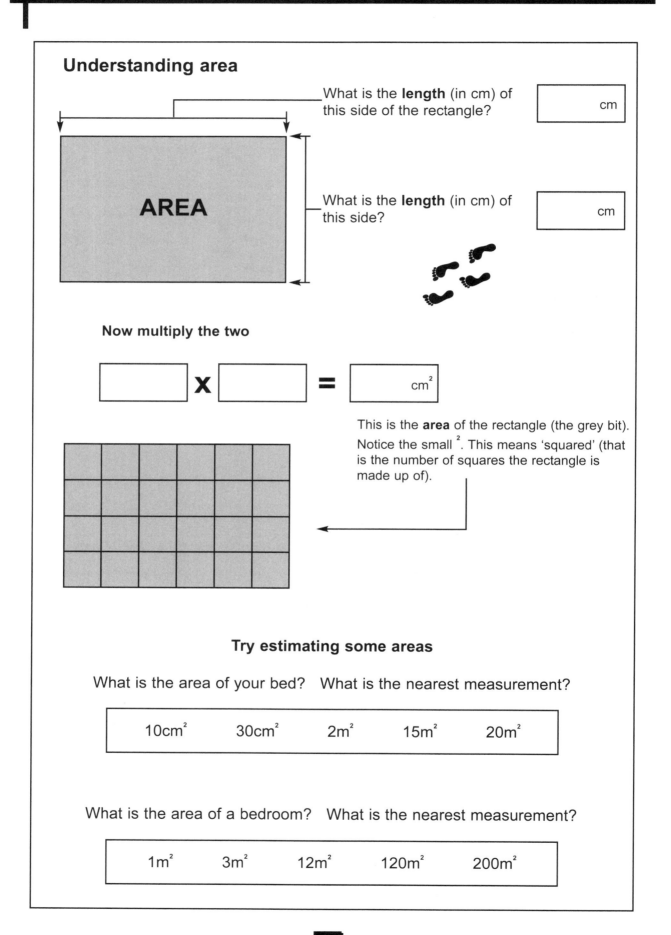

Understanding area

What is the **length** (in cm) of this side of the rectangle?

[ ] cm

AREA

What is the **length** (in cm) of this side?

[ ] cm

Now multiply the two

[ ] X [ ] = [ ] cm^2

This is the **area** of the rectangle (the grey bit). Notice the small ^{2}. This means 'squared' (that is the number of squares the rectangle is made up of).

Try estimating some areas

What is the area of your bed?   What is the nearest measurement?

10cm^2	30cm^2	2m^2	15m^2	20m^2

What is the area of a bedroom?   What is the nearest measurement?

1m^2	3m^2	12m^2	120m^2	200m^2

Getting to grips with area

Estimate the area of this page

$5cm^2$	$50cm^2$	$100cm^2$	$300cm^2$	$600cm^2$

Now calculate the area (in cm) of the page?

Calculate the area (in metres) of your classroom?

Calculate some large areas

What is the area (in metres) of the school hall?

What is the area (in metres) of a football pitch?

What is the area (in km) of Hyde Park in London? Use a map or the internet to help you.

What is the area (in km) of France?

What is the area of Scotland?

How many times would Scotland fit into France?

Solve It – area

Mrs Kofalot wants to buy a carpet for her bedroom which is a strange shape. The salesman tells her to measure the area of the room to work out how much carpet she needs to buy.

What is the area of Mrs Kofalot's bedroom?

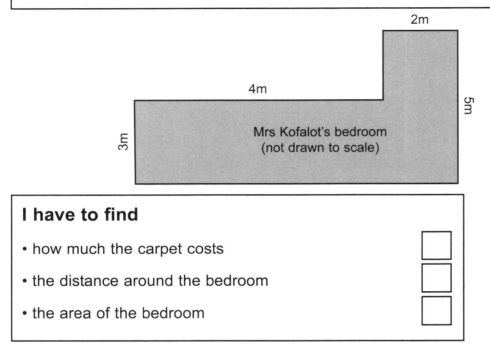

Mrs Kofalot's bedroom
(not drawn to scale)

2m

4m

3m

5m

I have to find

- how much the carpet costs ☐

- the distance around the bedroom ☐

- the area of the bedroom ☐

This means I have to

- add all of the sides together

- work out the area of each rectangle and add them together

- multiply the sides

My guess for the answer is

about 15 metres ☐

about 25 metres ☐

about 120 metres ☐

Here is my calculation

Use a calculator to check it

Getting to grips with perimeter

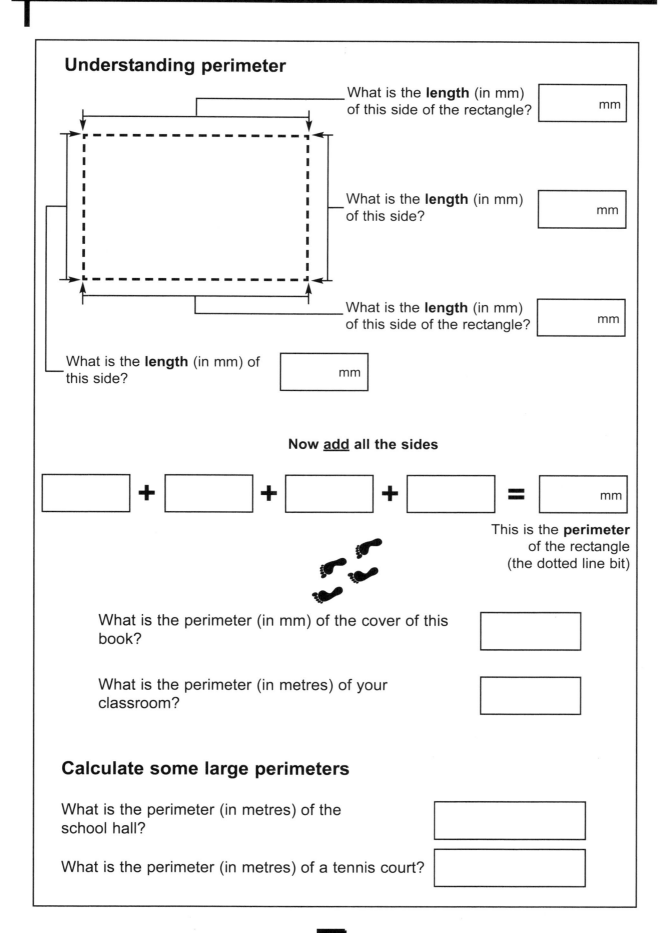

Understanding perimeter

What is the **length** (in mm) of this side of the rectangle? [ ] mm

What is the **length** (in mm) of this side? [ ] mm

What is the **length** (in mm) of this side of the rectangle? [ ] mm

What is the **length** (in mm) of this side? [ ] mm

Now <u>add</u> all the sides

[ ] **+** [ ] **+** [ ] **+** [ ] **=** [ ] mm

This is the **perimeter** of the rectangle (the dotted line bit)

What is the perimeter (in mm) of the cover of this book? [ ]

What is the perimeter (in metres) of your classroom? [ ]

Calculate some large perimeters

What is the perimeter (in metres) of the school hall? [ ]

What is the perimeter (in metres) of a tennis court? [ ]

Solve It – perimeter

Mr Minnesota has just bought a puppy. To keep it safe he needs to put a fence around the perimeter of his property.

What is the length of fencing that he needs to buy?

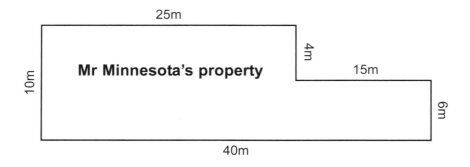

25m

4m

Mr Minnesota's property

15m

10m

6m

40m

I have to find

- the area of the property ☐
- the distance around the property ☐
- how much the fencing costs ☐

This means I have to

- add some of the sides together
- add all of the sides together
- multiply the sides

My guess for the answer is

about 50 metres ☐

about 100 metres ☐

about 900 metres ☐

Here is my calculation

Use a calculator to check it

Solve It – perimeter

Mrs Minnesota wants to paint the skirting boards in their living room. 1 pot of paint will be enough for 15 metres of skirting. She wants to know exactly how much paint to buy and she measures the perimeter of the room.

How many pots of paint will she need?

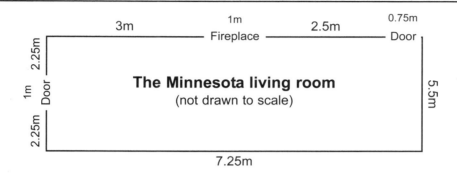

I have to find

- how much a pot of paint costs ☐

- the number of paint pots to paint required ☐

- the length of the skirting boards ☐

This means I have to

- add all of the sides together

- add all of the sides together and then take away where there is no skirting board

- multiply the sides

My guess for the answer is

about 15 metres ☐

about 20 metres ☐

about 35 metres ☐

Here is my calculation

Use a calculator to check it

Getting to grips with volume

Understanding volume

All containers (a cup, the kitchen sink, a bottle of water) have a capacity – or a volume that can go into the container.

A small bottle of water will have a volume in it of about 500 ml.

A large bottle of cola is usually 1 litre.

What is the volume of a teaspoon?
Which of the following is the nearest measurement?

| 1 ml | 5 ml | 50 ml | 100 ml | 150 ml |

How much water will fill a cup?
Which of the following is the nearest measurement?

| 1 ml | 5 ml | 200 ml | 1 litre | 10 litres |

What is the volume of a kitchen sink?
Which of the following is the nearest measurement?

| 1 ml | 5 ml | 200 ml | 1 litre | 10 litres |

Getting to grips with volume

Understanding volume

A box also has a volume and it is easy to work out the volume or capacity of the box.

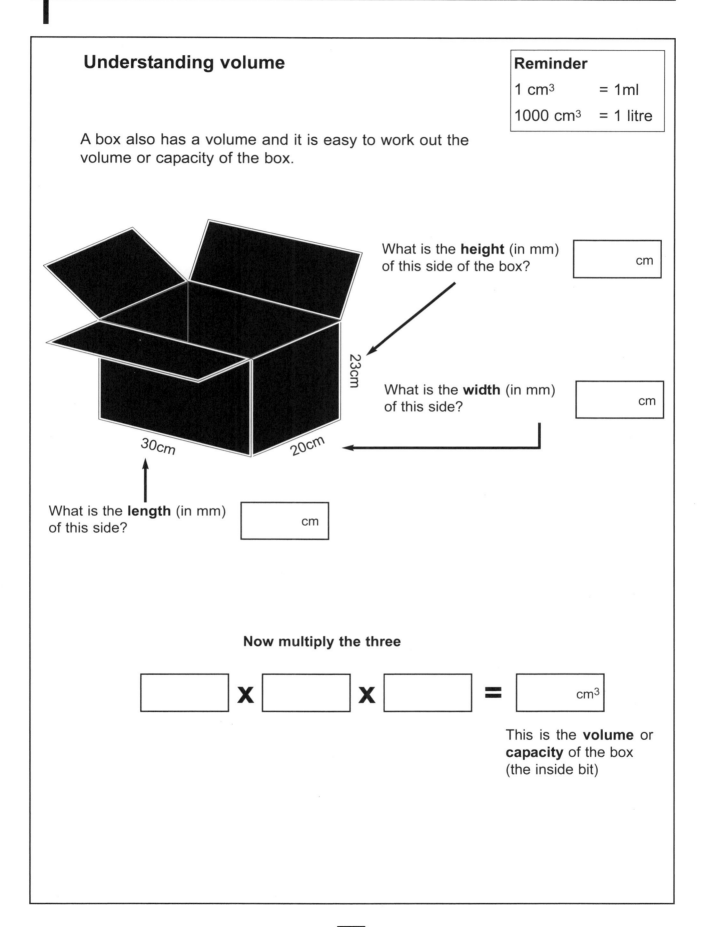

What is the **height** (in mm) of this side of the box?

cm

23cm

What is the **width** (in mm) of this side?

cm

30cm

20cm

What is the **length** (in mm) of this side?

cm

Now multiply the three

	X		X		=	cm³

This is the **volume** or **capacity** of the box (the inside bit)

Solve It – volume

You have a cough and the instruction on the 200ml medicine bottle is that you should take 15ml every three hours.

How many teaspoons is 15ml?

I have to find

- how many millilitres there are in a teaspoon ☐
- how much medicine there is in a bottle ☐
- how many teaspoons to have in a day ☐

This means I have to

- divide 200 by 15
- subtract 15 from 200
- divide 15 by the volume of a teaspoon

My guess for the answer is

about 13 ☐

about 3 ☐

about 4 ☐

Here is my calculation

Use a calculator to check it

Getting to grips with weight

Understanding weight

We usually measure how heavy things are in grams or kilograms. We would weigh something small (like a mobile phone) in grams, and something large and heavy (like a washing machine) in kilograms.

Try estimating the weight of things and then weigh them to see if you were right.

What does a mobile phone weigh?
Which of the following is the nearest measurement?

12g   40g   100g   250g   2kg

What does a cup of water weigh?
Which of the following is the nearest measurement?

2g   20g   200g   2kg   10kg

What does your school chair weigh?
Which of the following is the nearest measurement?

20g   200g   500g   4kg   20kg

Getting to grips with time

How long does it take you to get ready for school in the morning?
Which of the following is the nearest measurement?

30 seconds   1 minute   30 minutes   2 hours   3 hours

How long do you spend at school each day?
Which of the following is the nearest measurement?

20 minutes   3 hours   7 hours   20 hours

Reminder

60 seconds	=	1 minute
60 minutes	=	1 hour

Write $1\frac{1}{2}$ hours in minutes

Write 120 seconds in minutes

Write 220 minutes in hours and minutes

Solve It – time

You leave your house at 5.30pm and arrive at the airport at half past 7 in the evening.

How long did the journey take you?

I have to find

• how far it is to the airport ☐

• the time it takes to travel to the airport ☐

• the speed we had to travel ☐

This means I have to

• add the times together

• subtract one time from the other

• multiply the times together

My guess for the answer is

about 2 hours ☐

about 4 hours ☐

about 12 hours ☐

Here is my calculation

Use a calculator to check it

Solve It – time

You are going to watch a football match and leave home at 12.30pm. Unfortunately, the train is late and you get to the ground at 20 minutes past 3.

How long did the journey take you?

I have to find

- the time it took to travel to the ground ☐
- how late the train was ☐
- how far it is to the ground ☐

This means I have to

My guess for the answer is

about 50 minutes ☐

about 1 hours ☐

about 3 hours ☐

Here is my calculation

Use a calculator to check it

Solve It – time

You leave home to go to the shopping centre at 10.50am and arrive at 1.05pm.

How long did the journey take you?

I have to find

-

This means I have to

My guess for the answer is

about 55 minutes ☐

about 3 hours ☐

about 11 hours ☐

<u>Here is my calculation</u>

Use a calculator to check it

Resource sheets

Here are a variety of templates to copy and use to make up your own word problems.

Solve It

I have to		I have to find
•		•
•		•

My estimate

•

•

My calculation

• Check it •

Solve It –

I have to find

-
-
-

This means I have to

-

My guess for the answer is

Here is my calculation

Use a calculator to check it

Solve It –

Reminder

This means I have to

My guess for the answer is

Here is my calculation

How can you check it?

Here is my calculation

How can you check it?

Solve It –

I have to find

-
-
-

This means I have to

My answer is

Solve It –

I have to find

-
-
-

This means I have to

-
-
-

My guess for the answer is

Here is my calculation

Use a calculator to check it

Index